11·5·09

GOOD
&
BAD

Selfish

First published in 2007 by Cherrytree Books,
a division of the Evans Publishing Group
2A Portman Mansions
Chiltern St
London W1U 6NR

Design. D.R.ink

British Library Cataloguing in Publication Data
Amos, Janine
       Selfish – (Good & Bad Series)
       I. Title II. Green, Gwen III. Series
       179.8

ISBN 184234 397 1
13 –digit ISBN (from 1 Jan 2007) 978 1 84234 397 5

Selfish

By Janine Amos

Illustrated by Gwen Green

CHERRYTREE BOOKS

Jake's story

Jake and Harry were in the school play. They were going over their parts at Jake's house. Jake's mum was helping them.

"You've learnt all the words now," she said at last.

Just then, Jake's granddad arrived. He wanted to know all about it.

"We're Wealthy Princes!" said Jake. "But we don't know what to wear."

"We need long cloaks," said Harry. "I asked Miss James."

Jake looked around the room. "How about the curtains?" he asked, hopefully.

"No, you don't!" laughed his mum.

Jake's granddad was thinking hard. "I've got some clothes you can use," he said. "They're in a box somewhere. I'll find them for you."

"Great!" said Jake and Harry together.

The next day, Jake came home to find a big box.

"Your granddad left this," said Jake's mum. She handed him a note.

'Dear Wealthy Princes,' it said. 'Share these clothes between you. Love, Granddad.'

Jake and his mum lifted the lid. The box was full of beautiful costumes. Jake opened his eyes wide.

"Where did he get all this?" Jake asked, holding up a silvery jacket.

"Granddad used to be on the stage," said his mum, smiling. "Aren't you and Harry lucky?"

Jake nodded.

Jake and his mum sorted through the clothes. Jake wanted to wear everything!

"Don't forget Harry," said his mum. "Let's make two piles, one for each Prince."

The silver jacket went on to Jake's pile. He had a long purple cloak, too. And a hat with a curly feather.

Jake's mum went to make tea and Jake tried on his costume. Then he looked across to Harry's pile of clothes. Slowly, Jake picked up a golden cloak from Harry's pile. Then he tried on the trousers meant for Harry.

"I'll look magnificent!" said Jake to himself, as Harry's pile of clothes got smaller.

Harry came round later. Jake's costume was lying on the bed.

"I can't wait to try on our Prince clothes!" said Harry. He held up the golden cloak.

"Your costume's over there," said Jake. Jake pointed to a few clothes in the corner.

"That's not very much," said Harry, sadly. "You've got loads of things."

"He's my granddad," said Jake, looking away.

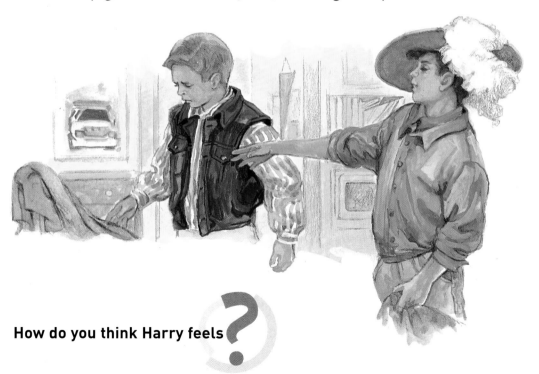

How do you think Harry feels

Soon it was the evening of the play. Jake's class was busy getting ready. Then Jake heard his name.

"Here's a visitor for you, Jake!" called Miss James.

It was Jake's granddad with a camera.

"I've come to take a photograph of the Wealthy Princes," he said.

Jake and Harry stood side by side for the photograph. Jake's costume sparkled and glittered. The feather in his hat bobbed up and down. But Jake's granddad was staring at Harry in his dull grey cloak.

Jake saw his granddad frown. And Jake went red.

What do you think Jake's granddad will say

"Come with me a minute, Jake," said Jake's granddad. Jake followed him to a corner of the room.

"Who are you, the Selfish Prince?" asked Jake's granddad.

Jake felt awful.

"I'm sorry," said Jake, quietly. "I just wanted to look magnificent."

"It's more important to be kind to other people," said his granddad. "Put yourself in Harry's shoes. Think how he feels."

Is Jake's granddad right?

Jake's mum and his granddad sat together in the audience. They clapped when Jake walked on stage. Then Jake's granddad started to smile. Jake was still wearing the silver jacket. But Harry had on the golden cloak and the green velvet trousers.

"Jake looks great!" whispered his mum.

"They both do!" smiled Jake's granddad. And he gave Jake a big wink.

Feeling like Jake

Jake didn't mean to be selfish. He just got carried away, thinking about himself. He forgot to think of Harry. Have you ever been selfish like Jake? Have you ever kept something for yourself instead of sharing it? When you like or want a thing very much, it's sometimes hard to remember to share.

Being selfish

Being selfish means thinking only about yourself. Selfish people don't think or care about others. They aren't much fun to be with. They make other people feel hurt or unimportant.

Other people's shoes

If you're tempted to be selfish, there's something you can do. Pretend you're standing in someone else's shoes. Try to understand how they feel. Understanding other people's feelings is a big step towards unselfishness.

Think about it

Read the stories in this book. Think about the people in the stories. You might feel like them sometimes. If you're tempted to be selfish like Jake, stop and think about the other person.

Laura's story

"The sea! The sea!" shouted Laura, pointing through the car window. "I saw it first!"

Laura was feeling happy. Her Aunty Jo was staying for a whole week. And Laura's mum was taking them for day trips in the car.

"What shall we do first?" asked Aunty Jo from the back seat. "How about finding a café?"

"No!" said Laura. "I want to go swimming!"

Laura's mum found a parking space. Laura grabbed her bag and swung open the car door.

"Come on!" she called. "Look at the waves!"

Laura went running down to the sea. Laura's mum and Aunty Jo followed behind.

Soon they were playing in the sea. Laura had a beach ball.

"Catch this!" she called, throwing the ball.

They played for a long time. Then Laura's mum started to puff.

"I'm worn out!" she laughed, and she flopped down on to the sand.

"Me, too," said Aunty Jo. She picked up her book.

"Don't read!" said Laura. "I want to do something. I want to see the model village."

The model village was fun. There were tiny houses, a church and a school. Laura peeped in at the windows. She pretended she was a giant.

"I need a cup of coffee now," said Aunty Jo at last.

"But I want to see the aquarium next!" wailed Laura.

At the café, Laura had a milkshake. She drank it quickly. Laura's mum and Aunty Jo were talking. Laura kicked her legs against the chair. Bang, bang, bang went Laura.

"Hurry up!" she said. "I'm bored."

Laura's mum gave her a cross look, as Aunty Jo swallowed down her hot coffee.

How do you think Laura's mum and Aunty Jo feel?

Outside the sun was shining.

"Let's go for a walk along the cliff," said Aunty Jo.

Laura screwed up her face. "I'm tired," she moaned.

"We'll make it a short walk," Aunty Jo laughed. But she didn't look happy.

Soon Laura had a stone in her shoe. Then she felt something in her eye. She sat down on a rock.

"Walking's boring," said Laura. "It's time for the aquarium."

There were crowds of people at the aquarium. They were watching the big shark.

"It's hot in here!" said Laura's mum. Aunty Jo had to take off her jumper.

But they waited while Laura looked at all the fish.

Then it was time to eat. There was a restaurant nearby.

Laura's mum checked the menu. "This looks fine," she said. "There's plenty to choose from."

"It's not fine," said Laura walking on, "because I want a Chinese!"

Aunty Jo took hold of Laura's arm. She put her face very close to Laura's.

"We always have to do what you want! It's my holiday too, remember!" said Aunty Jo. "You don't care about anyone else," she went on. "It's no fun being with you. You're selfish and bossy!"

Laura didn't answer. She just stared at her feet.

Laura ate her meal quietly. She was quiet all the way home, too. She was thinking about what Aunty Jo had said.

How do you think Laura feels

At bathtime, Laura's mum stayed for a chat.

"Do you think I'm selfish and bossy?" Laura asked.

"Sometimes," said her mum. "Sometimes you want everything your own way. You forget to think of others."

Laura looked sad. "If I really try, do you think I can change?" she asked.

"Yes," said her mum. "And you can start right now. You can ask Aunty Jo what she'd like to do tomorrow."

"That's a good idea!" said Laura, smiling.

Selfish like Laura

Laura was bossy and selfish. She knew what she wanted to do. And she expected her mum and Aunty Jo to do exactly what she said. She didn't care what they wanted. People who behave like Laura aren't fun to be with. They spoil things for everyone else.

Taking turns

It's important to know your own mind. And it's important to do things that you enjoy. But other people need a turn, too. That's only fair. If you're sharing a day with someone else, remember to ask what they'd like to do. Take it in turns to choose what to do next.

Danny's story

Danny was going to the fair! He was going with his mum. Danny's mum liked all the scary rides. They always had a great time.

"Are you ready yet?" Danny asked for the third time.

"Nearly!" smiled Danny's mum. She picked up the telephone. "I just need to speak to Aunty Charlene. She's not very well."

When Danny's mum put down the 'phone, she was frowning.

"Your aunty's in hospital," she told Danny. "So Josh is coming with us. His dad's bringing him here now."

Josh was Danny's cousin.

"He'll spoil everything!" complained Danny. "He's too small for half the rides!"

"Don't be mean," said Danny's mum.

Danny sat down to wait.

As soon as Josh arrived, they set off.

The entrance to the fair was crowded.

"Make sure we don't lose each other!" warned Danny's mum.

Danny reached for her hand. But Josh was already holding it.

Danny looked up at the Big Wheel. He wanted to ride on it, but it was very high. The Helter Skelter looked fun too.

"Let's go on something!" said Danny.

"OK," said his mum. "Let's go on the Teacups. They have three seats."

Danny, his mum and Josh twisted round in a Teacup. But it wasn't fast enough for Danny.

Next, they went on the Water Shute. It shot up and down, and dipped right into the water. Whoosh!

Josh gripped the handrail tight. But it wasn't scary enough for Danny.

The Ghost Train was better. Witches jumped out from dark cupboards. A cobweb flew in Danny's face. And a skeleton danced in front of them.

Danny grinned at his mum. But she had her arms round Josh. He was hiding his head in her lap.

How do you think Danny feels

"What next?" asked Danny's mum.

"I'm sick of baby rides!" said Danny. "I want you to come on the Big Wheel with me."

"But what about Josh?" said his mum.

"Who cares?" shouted Danny. And he stamped his foot.

Josh started to cry.

Danny's mum gave Josh a hug. Then she helped him on to a roundabout. Josh was soon smiling again.

Danny's mum turned to look at Danny.

What do you think Danny's mum will say?

"You're being selfish, Danny," said his mum. "Josh is too little to go on every ride. You know that. And we can't leave him to wait on his own."

"But you're my mum. I want you to come with me," said Danny.

"You can't have me all to yourself," said Danny's mum, gently. "I know it's hard. But today we're looking after Josh."

Danny put his head down. He kicked at an empty crisp packet.
His mum carried on talking.

"Josh's mum is in hospital, remember?" she said. "Try to think
how he's feeling."

Danny thought.

"He must be a bit sad," he said after a while.

Danny looked up at the Big Wheel.

"You can still go on some of the big things, Danny," said his mum.
"But you'll have to go by yourself."

"OK," nodded Danny.

Josh soon finished on the roundabout.

"Will you watch me, if I go on something?" asked Danny.

"Of course we will!" said his mum.

The Big Wheel looked too big for Danny on his own. He chose the Helter Skelter.

From the very top, the people on the ground seemed tiny.

Danny took a deep breath. He searched for his mum and Josh. There they were, waving to him!

"Whee!" went Danny, as he skidded down. The Helter Skelter was fast and scary. Danny thought it was great!

Feeling like Danny

Danny didn't like sharing his mum. He wanted her all to himself. But that was selfish – Josh needed her, too. Have you ever felt like Danny?

Sharing someone

Sharing someone you love can be hard. It can be much harder than sharing sweets or toys. But it's all part of growing up. Sometimes, even adults are selfish about the people they love.

Being unselfish

Danny didn't get what he wanted. He had to give up going on the Big Wheel with his mum. But he had fun on the Helter Skelter instead. Danny learnt to be unselfish. He learnt to think of someone else's feelings. And he learnt that you can have a good time and be unselfish, too.

Thinking about it

Jake, Laura and Danny were all selfish. And they each learnt something about selfishness. Think about the stories in this book. What have you learnt about selfishness – and about being unselfish?

If you are feeling frightened or unhappy, don't keep it to yourself. Talk to an adult you can trust, like a parent or a teacher. If you feel really alone, you could telephone or write to one of these offices. Remember, there is always someone who can help.

Childline
Freephone 0800 1111
Address: Freepost 1111, London N1 0BR
www.childline.org.uk

Childline for children in care
Freephone 0800 884444 (6 - 10pm)

NSPCC Child Protection Line
Freephone 0808 8005000
www.nspcc.org.uk

The Samaritans
08457 909090
www.samaritans.org.uk